INSIDE MLB

SAN FRANCISCO GIANTS

BY DOUGLAS CARL

SportsZone

An Imprint of Abdo Publishing
abdobooks.com

abdobooks.com

Published by Abdo Publishing, a division of ABDO, PO Box 398166, Minneapolis, Minnesota 55439.

Printed in the United States of America, North Mankato, Minnesota.
102022
012023

THIS BOOK CONTAINS RECYCLED MATERIALS

Cover Photo: Thearon W. Henderson/Getty Images Sport/Getty Images
Interior Photos: William Purnell/Icon Sportswire/AP Images, 4; Matt Slocum/AP Images, 6; AP Images, 8, 18, 22; Transcendental Graphics/Getty Images Sport/Getty Images, 10; Mark Rucker/Transcendental Graphics/Getty Images Sport/Getty Images, 13; Bruce Bennett Studios/Getty Images Studios/Getty Images, 14; Bettmann/Getty Images, 16; New York Daily News Archive/Getty Images, 21; Tom Gallagher/New York Daily News Archive/Getty Images, 23; Archive Photos/Getty Images, 24; MLB Photos/Hulton Archive/Getty Images, 27; Tony Tomsic/AP Images, 29; George Gojkovich/Getty Images Sport/Getty Images, 30; News Base/AP Images, 33; Harry How/Allsport/Getty Images Sport/Getty Images, 34; Lance Iversen/San Francisco Chronicle/AP Images, 37; Kyle Ericson/AP Images, 39; Bill Nichols/AP Images, 40; Derek Tuskan/AP Images, 41

Editor: Steph Giedd
Series Designer: Becky Daum

Library of Congress Control Number: 2022940496

Publisher's Cataloging-in-Publication Data

Names: Carl, Douglas, author.
Title: San Francisco Giants / by Douglas Carl
Description: Minneapolis, Minnesota: Abdo Publishing, 2023 | Series: Inside MLB | Includes online resources and index.
Identifiers: ISBN 9781098290313 (lib. bdg.) | ISBN 9781098275518 (ebook)
Subjects: LCSH: San Francisco Giants (Baseball team)--Juvenile literature. | Baseball teams--Juvenile literature. | Professional sports--Juvenile literature. | Sports franchises--Juvenile literature. | Major League Baseball (Organization)--Juvenile literature.
Classification: DDC 796.35764--dc23

TABLE OF

CONTENTS

SHOULDERS OF GIANTS

One out away from winning the 2014 World Series, San Francisco Giants pitcher Madison Bumgarner allowed a single. The Kansas City Royals were still alive in Game 7. Bumgarner had already played a starring role in the Series. The Giants' ace had started and dominated in two wins over Kansas City. But in Game 7, Bumgarner was called on to finish the job.

The Giants had taken a 3–2 lead in the fourth inning. With starter Jeremy Affeldt tiring, manager Bruce Bochy turned to Bumgarner in the fifth. Bumgarner had just pitched three days earlier. But he'd been their best pitcher all year.

Bumgarner allowed a hit to the first batter he saw. He then retired the next 14. But with the score still 3–2, the Royals

Madison Bumgarner delivers a pitch during Game 1 of the 2014 World Series.

Bumgarner, *left*, and catcher Buster Posey celebrate the Giants' 2014 World Series title.

attempted a comeback in the ninth. Alex Gordon ended up on third base after his single to center was misplayed in the outfield. That put the tying run on third base with two outs. Now Bumgarner had to contend with Salvador Pérez.

Bumgarner had thrown 62 pitches. And Pérez was hanging tough and keeping the game alive. Finally, Bumgarner got Pérez to hit a pop fly. Giants third baseman Pablo Sandoval ran into foul territory to make the catch. The Giants' ace had become the reliever they needed to lock down another World Series title.

BIG APPLE BASEBALL

The first real World Series was still 20 years away in 1883. That was the year the New York Gothams began play on a former polo field as members of the National League (NL). The Gothams took their name from a nickname for New York City. But as early as 1885, the team began to be known as the Giants. Exactly why remains a mystery.

One story goes that the nickname came from manager Jim Mutrie. After an exciting comeback win in 1885, the story says, he praised his team by saying, "My big fellows, my giants."

However the Giants got their name, they soon lived up to it. The Giants won back-to-back NL championships in 1888 and 1889. Both years featured an early version of the World Series.

Giants manager John McGraw was nicknamed "Little Napoleon" due to the aggressive tactics he encouraged as a manager.

The Giants won both championship playoffs. In 1889 they beat a team from Brooklyn that would later be known as the Dodgers. It was an early showdown between teams that would become longtime rivals.

McGRAW ARRIVES

The Giants spent much of their early years moving around. In 1889 alone they played in three different stadiums. In 1891 they finally found a permanent home. The Giants moved into the Polo Grounds in Upper Manhattan and stayed there for more than 60 years.

By 1902 the Giants were at the very bottom of the NL. They finished 53 1/2 games back of first place that year. Something had to change.

John McGraw had been playing for and managing the Baltimore Orioles of the American League (AL). But the fiery, competitive McGraw often clashed with AL president Ban Johnson and wanted out. He took the Giants job in July of 1902, looking to turn them around as the team's third manager that season.

McGraw had a great influence on the Giants and on the sport of baseball. His players were aggressive runners and stole a lot of bases. He employed pinch runners and relief pitchers more than other managers of his era did. He valued pitching and defense and had strict standards of who he thought would fit on the team.

SEEING THE SIGNS

John McGraw was one of the most influential managers in baseball history. He was accidentally responsible for popularizing the use of hand signals in baseball. In 1902 the Giants had pitcher Luther Taylor, who was deaf. To help teammates communicate with him, McGraw made the whole team learn sign language. The Giants eventually started signing to each other during games, leading to the signs seen today.

Right-handed ace Christy Mathewson won at least 30 games four times in his Giants' career, including a career-high 37 in 1908.

McGraw's biggest star was ace pitcher Christy Mathewson. The right-hander helped set the standard for modern starting pitchers with his power and control. Mathewson's name is still atop the Giants' leaderboards on most major pitching records.

While Mathewson embarrassed hitters on the mound, he did so in a calm and courteous way. He was known for his good sportsmanship in a time when baseball could still be rough and wild. Even non-Giants fans enjoyed watching "the Gentleman's Hurler."

ATOP THE NL

The Giants were back on top of the NL by 1904. By then the World Series had formed so that teams from the NL and AL could compete to determine who was greatest. But McGraw considered the AL to be a minor league. And he still despised Johnson. So the Giants refused to play in the 1904 World Series.

By 1905 McGraw had changed his mind. After repeating as NL champs, the Giants took on the Philadelphia Athletics in the World Series. Mathewson dominated, pitching three shutouts to lead a 4–1 series win.

McGraw's Giants were a force. They won 10 NL titles in a 21-season span between 1904 and 1924. However, it took a long time to win another World Series.

MERKLE'S ERROR

In 1908 the Giants were involved in one of the most famous mistakes in baseball history. That year the Giants dueled with the Chicago Cubs for the NL pennant. In a late-season game, Giants rookie Fred Merkle failed to advance to second on what should have been the game-winning hit. He turned to head back to the dugout, thinking the game was over. The Cubs tagged second, and Merkle was ruled out. As a result, the Giants had to play a one-game playoff with the Cubs at the end of the season, which New York lost.

The Giants lost close series in 1911, 1912, 1913, and 1917. In 1921 the Giants faced the New York Yankees, who were led by slugger Babe Ruth. The matchup between McGraw and Ruth was a battle of different baseball beliefs. McGraw still hated the AL. And he didn't like players such as Ruth who relied on home runs instead of the aggressive base running and defense.

At first it appeared that Ruth and the Yankees would have the last laugh as they went up 2–0. But the Giants came back to win Games 3 and 4. After a Game 5 Yankees win, Ruth was lost to injury for the rest of the nine-game series. The Giants went on to win three in a row and capture their second World Series title.

The Giants repeated as champs in 1922. They did it by defeating Ruth and the Yankees in five games. McGraw also led the Giants to the 1923 and 1924 World Series, but they fell short both years.

McGraw's Giants were almost always winners. But after making it to the World Series in 1924, McGraw never won another NL title. By 1932 the team had slipped to its worst finish in nearly two decades.

During that season, McGraw decided to retire. He was in poor health and was frustrated with not winning more. It was the end of a historically successful era. McGraw managed 31 NL seasons and two AL seasons, still the most in history.

And his 2,763 career wins were a record when he retired. The Giants had a huge hole to fill.

Yankees star Babe Ruth attempts to slide into second during the 1922 World Series. Giants infielder George Kelly, *third from left*, moves to tag him out.

NEW YORK

CHAPTER 2

REIGNING IN NEW YORK

The loss of beloved manager John McGraw in 1932 sent the Giants tumbling. But the season was not a total loss. It was the first year that outfielder Mel Ott led the NL in home runs.

Ott stood just 5 feet, 9 inches tall. But his small frame held big power. He clubbed 38 homers in 1932 on his way to becoming the first NL player to hit 500 in a career.

Ott's total dipped to 23 the next year. In 1933 it was pitching that fueled a surprising Giants' run at the NL title. Ace Carl Hubbell led the NL in wins, earned-run average (ERA), and shutouts. The left-hander was known best for his deadly screwball. He was named the NL's Most Valuable Player (MVP).

Power-hitter Mel Ott led the NL in homers a total of six times during his 22-year career with the Giants.

Lefty Carl Hubbell was known for his targeted control and a wicked screwball.

Under new manager Bill Terry, who was also the team's first baseman, the Giants won the pennant.

The Giants leaned on Hubbell in the World Series against the Washington Senators. The ace won both of his starts, pitching 20 innings and allowing zero earned runs. Ott boosted the offense, picking up seven hits, including a two-run homer in Game 1.

The Giants built a 3–1 series lead. In Game 5, New York built a 3–0 lead in the sixth inning. But the Senators tied it up against starter Hal Schumacher in the bottom of the inning. Unable to get the final out, Schumacher was replaced by 43-year-old Dolf Luque.

HALL OF FAME SHUTDOWN

MLB's All-Star Game features the best players in baseball playing against each other. The 1934 All-Star Game featured more star power than most, with 28 future Hall of Famers taking the field in New York that day. Carl Hubbell was one of them, pitching on his own field. Hubbell got the best of his fellow legends. At one point, he struck out five future Hall of Famers in a row by fanning Babe Ruth, Lou Gehrig, Jimmie Foxx, Al Simmons, and Joe Cronin.

The unlikely hero tossed 4 1/3 shutout innings that day to keep the Senators off the scoreboard. In the top of the 10th, Ott blasted a solo home run to deep center. Luque allowed two runners in the bottom of the 10th before finishing the job. The Giants were champions again.

THE SHOT HEARD 'ROUND THE WORLD

Hubbell won the MVP Award again in 1936 as the Giants won another NL pennant. But they went on to lose in six games to

Bobby Thomson, *top right, hand raised,* is mobbed by teammates as he reaches home plate after hitting "the Shot Heard 'round the World."

the New York Yankees. Terry retired as a player after that but led the Giants back to the World Series in 1937. They again fell to the mighty Yankees.

As the careers of Ott and Hubbell wound down, the Giants began to struggle. They suffered mostly losing seasons throughout the 1940s. In a surprising turn of events, the Giants' biggest rival had a hand in turning the team around. Manager Leo Durocher left the Brooklyn Dodgers during the 1948 season to come across town and manage the Giants.

As a player, Durocher was known as "the Lip" for his habit of arguing with umpires. He kept up the habit as a manager and frequently got into trouble. But players and fans appreciated his passion. And it helped that he won a lot of games.

By 1951 the Giants were back in the thick of the pennant race. Durocher won Manager of the Year. The team also had veteran stars leading the way in outfielders Monte Irvin and Bobby Thomson. They also had a star rookie center fielder in Willie Mays. On the mound, pitchers Sal Maglie and Larry Jansen each won 23 games.

After a slow start, the Giants rallied from 13 1/2 games back in August to stun the Dodgers and force a three-game playoff series to decide the NL pennant. The Giants and Dodgers split the first two games. Whoever won Game 3 at the Polo Grounds would win the NL. It looked as if it was over for the Giants, who trailed 4–1 going to the bottom of the ninth.

The Giants, though, began to rally. After Whitey Lockman's double made it 4–2, Thomson stepped up with two runners on. On the second pitch he saw from the Dodgers' Ralph Branca, Thomson hit a line drive home run to left. The walk-off blast would become known as "the Shot Heard 'round the World."

SAY HEY

Thomson's home run was the highlight of the season, as the Giants lost to the Yankees in the World Series. But it was one of the youngest stars on the 1951 team who soon became the face of the Giants.

Mays was just 20 that season, when he was named NL Rookie of the Year. Two years later, he missed the entire season while serving in the military. But Mays never saw combat. In fact, he spent most of his time playing on the Army baseball team. He was in prime shape when he returned to the Giants in 1954.

With Mays the Giants improved by 27 wins. The "Say Hey Kid," who earned the name by greeting everyone with "Hey" as a rookie, led the NL with a .345 batting average while hitting 41 homers. Mays also made his first of 20 consecutive All-Star teams and won his first of two MVP Awards.

Durocher once said that he would still think Mays was the best player ever, even if another player hit .450 and stole 100 bases. Mays had a rare combination of speed, power, and defense. He was also a famously enthusiastic and positive player who was beloved by teammates and fans.

Mays's MVP year led the Giants back to the NL pennant in 1954. And his signature moment came in the outfield during Game 1 of the 1954 World Series against Cleveland.

Willie Mays makes "the Catch" in Game 1 of the 1954 World Series.

The game was tied 2–2 in the top of the eighth. Cleveland slugger Vic Wertz came up with two on and crushed a ball to deep center. Mays took off at a sprint, his back to the infield. He never turned around, tracking the ball over his shoulder until it settled in his glove, 425 feet (130 m) from home plate. It's known today simply as "the Catch." The Giants swept Cleveland in four games to recapture a championship.

The Giants drew only 11,606 fans to their final game at the Polo Grounds in 1957.

WESTBOUND

Even as the Giants were winning the World Series, there were rumors they might be on the move. Owner Horace Stoneham had been trying to get a new stadium to replace the aging Polo Grounds for years. But nobody knew how far he was willing to go.

Stoneham believed that with three teams in New York—including the Brooklyn Dodgers and New York Yankees—his team could not compete financially without a new stadium. The Dodgers were in a similar position. The crosstown rivals soon found homes across the country.

In the summer of 1957, Stoneham announced that the Giants were moving to San Francisco. Meanwhile, the Dodgers were off to Los Angeles, and the two teams became the first MLB teams in California. The Giants left behind loyal fans and a legendary history as they began a new era of baseball.

Giants owner Horace Stoneham, *right*, boards a plane with Dodgers owner Walter O'Malley to attend a meeting to move their franchises to California.

SAN FRANCIS

BAY AREA BALL

California baseball was something of an experiment. But the Giants had a great chance to succeed. They brought baseball's best player with them.

Willie Mays was frequently in the running for MVP. His star power meant the Giants frequently drew big crowds. But the Giants were not a one-man team. In 1958 and 1959, they had back-to-back Rookie of the Year winners in future superstars Orlando Cepeda and Willie McCovey.

Moving didn't solve all the Giants' problems. They still did not have a new stadium right away. They had to play their first two seasons in a minor league park while their new home was being built.

The Giants moved west with a star-filled lineup, led by center fielder Willie Mays.

CROIX DE CANDLESTICK

Fans who attended night games at Candlestick Park often braved cold and windy conditions. Starting in 1983, the team handed out pins to recognize fans who stayed until the end of extra-inning home games. The pins read *Croix de Candlestick*, with *croix* meaning "cross," as in a symbol of bravery for the award. The pins also had the Latin phrase "*Veni, vidi, vixi.*" on the bottom, meaning "I came, I saw, I survived."

Candlestick Park finally opened in 1960. The stadium had all the amenities fans were looking for. But it became best known for its cold conditions, especially at night. Located on a point jutting out into San Francisco Bay, Candlestick's swirling winds and chilly nights were a challenge for both players and fans. A strong breeze at the first of two 1961 All-Star Games knocked Giants pitcher Stu Miller off balance as he tried to deliver a ball.

SAN FRANCISCO SERIES

While fans endured frosty nights at the ballpark, they also enjoyed winning baseball. Mays led the NL with 49 homers in 1962 as the Giants dueled the Los Angeles Dodgers for the NL title. Much as in 1951, the teams ended up tying and playing a three-game playoff series.

Once again, the teams split the first two games. Game 3 was decided in the final inning. The Giants trailed 4–2 going into

Orlando Cepeda had career highs of 46 home runs and 142 RBIs during the 1961 season.

the top of the ninth. A single and two walks loaded the bases. Mays and Cepeda then drove in the tying runs. The Giants then loaded the bases for All-Star Jim Davenport. His walk drove in the go-ahead run. San Francisco added one more in a 6–4 victory.

The first San Francisco World Series featured a familiar opponent. For the seventh time, it was the Giants against the New York Yankees. And like the previous four meetings, it was the Yankees coming out on top. The Giants lost Game 7 in heartbreaking fashion 1–0.

THE DARK AGES

The 1962 season was the last World Series in nearly three decades for the Giants. Despite having several stars, the team did not reach the postseason again for 25 years.

However, the Giants still had Mays. And on September 22, 1969, he became just the second player in MLB history to reach 600 home runs. Early in the 1972 season, Mays left the Giants after 21 seasons with the team.

Other bright spots included pitchers Gaylord Perry and Juan Marichal. Perry threw a no-hitter, and Marichal used his famous high-leg-kick delivery to delight fans across 14 seasons. Pitcher Mike McCormick won the first Cy Young Award in Giants history as the best pitcher in the league in 1967.

But most often, Giants talent was heading out rather than coming in. Perry, Marichal, and McCormick's contracts were all sold or traded away by the 1970s. While the Giants piled up losses off the field, there were rumors the team could be on the move again. In 1976 the Giants very nearly relocated to Toronto. Instead, that city got an expansion team of its own.

"The Dominican Dandy" Juan Marichal baffled hitters with his high leg kick and pinpoint control.

BUILDING UP

The Giants' dark era reached its bottom with a 100-loss season in 1985. They'd never done that before in 102 years of baseball. It prompted more trades.

In came veteran stars like outfielders Kevin Mitchell and Candy Maldonado, as well as pitchers Dave Dravecky and Rick Reuschel. Other talent came up through the minors, including first baseman Will "the Thrill" Clark, second baseman Robby Thompson, and third baseman Matt Williams.

All these players helped San Francisco turn things around quickly. The Giants won the NL West in 1987. Two years later, they won the division again as Mitchell was named the NL MVP. San Francisco then knocked off the Chicago Cubs in the NL

Kevin Mitchell's MVP season of 1989 was his only year with over 40 home runs or 100 RBIs.

Championship Series (NLCS). The Giants were back in the World Series for the first time since 1962.

BATTLE OF THE BAY

The Giants faced another familiar opponent in the World Series. Right across the San Francisco Bay were the Oakland Athletics. And in 1989, they were the best team in baseball.

Oakland was expected to win and pitched two of the AL's best starters, Dave Stewart and Mike Moore, in Games 1 and 2. The A's won both games in Oakland, and the series moved across the Bay to Candlestick. A big crowd was waiting for the first World Series game in San Francisco in 27 years.

As the teams were warming up for Game 3, the ground began to shake. An earthquake struck California's central coast just after 5 p.m. and did major damage across the region. The game was postponed a short time later.

After players and fans left the stadium, they saw the devastation across the Bay Area. It was unclear if the World Series would resume at all. The quake killed 63 people and caused more than $6 billion in damage.

As the area slowly recovered, people were hoping to see some baseball as a distraction. Game 3 took place 10 days later at Candlestick. Oakland was able to throw its top two starters again, and the A's swept a series overshadowed by one of the biggest disasters in California history.

SAVING SAN FRANCISCO BASEBALL

The World Series run didn't stop the Giants' latest relocation rumors. Giants owner Bob Lurie insisted the team needed to get out of cold, aging Candlestick. And by 1992, a new city emerged in search of a team.

St. Petersburg, Florida, had built a new stadium in hopes of a team moving there. Lurie was willing to sell the team to someone else in San Francisco who could get a stadium built. But nobody was buying, so Lurie reached an agreement to move the Giants in time for the 1993 season. It was front-page news in Florida.

However, the deal was not approved by the NL. At the last minute, a group led by San Francisco businessman Peter Magowan made a better offer. The NL accepted, and the Giants stayed. Magowan's group wasted no time turning the Giants around. One of their first big moves was to sign superstar outfielder Barry Bonds. He was the reigning MVP.

Bonds possessed a rare blend of speed and power. His father, Bobby, had been a similar player for the Giants in the 1960s and 1970s. Willie Mays was another huge influence on Bonds. The Giants' great was even Bonds's godfather.

Bonds won a second consecutive MVP Award in 1993, his first year in San Francisco. He led the NL in homers and runs batted in (RBIs). The Giants won 103 games and were in the NL West race until the season's final day.

Bonds was a historically good player. In 1998 he became the first player to reach 400 career homers and 400 stolen bases. Magowan may have written the check to keep the Giants in San Francisco. But Bonds made them a wise investment.

After seven seasons and two MVP Awards with the Pittsburgh Pirates, Barry Bonds signed with the Giants in December 1992.

San Francisco
GIANTS
25

EVEN YEAR MAGIC

Despite the historic achievements of Barry Bonds, the Giants reached the playoffs only once in the 1990s. However, the Giants opened a brand-new downtown ballpark in 2000, ensuring they would play in San Francisco for years to come.

The first year in the park saw Bonds finish second in MVP voting to teammate Jeff Kent. But in 2001, Bonds was a one-man show. He ran away with the MVP Award by hitting home runs at a historic pace.

The single-season home-run record of 70 had been set just three years earlier by St. Louis Cardinals first baseman

Barry Bonds celebrates his record-setting 71st home run of the 2001 season with his teammates and his son, Nikolai.

Mark McGwire. Bonds went into the season's final series in San Francisco tied with McGwire.

On a Friday night against the Los Angeles Dodgers, Bonds blasted two homers to become the new home-run king. He added a 73rd that Sunday, but it wasn't enough to get the Giants into the playoffs.

WALKS TO REMEMBER

Barry Bonds was one of the most feared hitters in MLB history. In one 1998 game, the Arizona Diamondbacks chose to walk Bonds with the bases loaded rather than risk him hitting a grand slam. Bonds's walk totals were a major reason why he never hit more than 50 homers after his 73 in 2001. Bonds was intentionally walked an MLB-record 688 times in his career. That is more than double the total of second place. Bonds is the all-time walks leader as well.

BACK IN THE SERIES

The 2002 season was a different story as another MVP season from Bonds boosted the team into an NL wild-card spot. Despite failing to win the West, the Giants went on a run in the playoffs, knocking off the Atlanta Braves and Cardinals to reach the World Series.

Facing the surprising Anaheim Angels, the Giants fell behind 2–1 in the series before rallying to go up 3–2. The Giants led 5–0 in the seventh inning of Game 6, just nine outs from their first World Series victory since moving from New York.

But then the Angels rallied. Giants reliever Félix Rodríguez allowed a three-run homer in the seventh. Then star closer Robb Nen allowed the go-ahead run in the eighth. The Giants were stunned but had another chance to win in Game 7. Instead, they managed just a single run and lost the series.

BARRY'S HOME-RUN CHASE

The Giants didn't reach the playoffs for the rest of Bonds's career. And the slugger never approached 73 homers again. But he was consistently moving up the all-time leaderboard. He passed Mays with his 661st in 2004. That year he won his seventh MVP Award, by far the most in history. By 2007 he was nearing all-time leader Hank Aaron's 755.

Bonds connects on his all-time record 756th home run against the Washington Nationals on August 7, 2007.

Apart from Giants fans, however, few others were

cheering Bonds on. Though he had never failed a test, Bonds was rumored to be a user of performance-enhancing drugs that allowed him to hit more home runs.

Drugs or not, Bonds became the greatest home-run hitter of all time on August 7, 2007. But after the Giants concluded a third losing season in a row, they opted not to re-sign Bonds to a new contract. The team wanted to get younger, even if it meant parting with a legend.

A NEW ERA

The 2008 Giants had a young pitching staff. One of those promising young players was pitcher Tim Lincecum, who won the first Giants Cy Young Award in more than 40 years. The shaggy-haired righty was a strikeout master who won another Cy Young in 2009.

The 2009 season also saw third baseman Pablo Sandoval develop into a reliable hitter with power. Debuting that same year was catcher Buster Posey, though he had his first full season in 2010. He immediately became one of the best catchers in the game and won Rookie of the Year for his efforts in his first season with the Giants.

Despite trailing most of the year, the Giants rallied to overtake the San Diego Padres and win the West on the season's final day. A mix of young stars and reliable veterans then led the Giants on a run to the World Series against the Texas Rangers.

Lincecum got the Giants off to a great start with a win in Game 1. Giants pitchers shut out the Rangers in Game 2 and Game 4 as they took a 3–1 series lead. Lincecum took the mound again in Game 5 ready to finish off the series and secure a World Series championship for his team.

Tim Lincecum led the NL in strikeouts every year from 2008 to 2010.

The ace was dominant yet again. But the Giants' offense needed some help. Shortstop Édgar Rentería had hit just three homers in the regular season. But he came to the plate in the seventh inning and crushed his second of the series, a three-run blast. That was all the offense the Giants needed. Star closer Brian Wilson came on to record the save, and San Francisco had its long-awaited title.

Buster Posey became the first NL catcher to win the league's batting title since 1942 when he hit .336 in 2012.

DYNASTY

The Giants were far from done. While Posey developed into an MVP by 2012, it was the pitching staff that kept San Francisco among the league's best. Starter Matt Cain pitched a perfect game during the 2012 season. He was joined in the rotation by Lincecum, Madison Bumgarner, Ryan Vogelsong, and Barry Zito as the Giants reached the World Series again.

Against the Detroit Tigers, Sandoval was nearly a one-man offense. The fan favorite slugger hit three homers in Game 1 and went on to win series MVP. Cain, Bumgarner, Vogelsong, and Zito worked magic on the mound. Giants pitchers allowed just six total runs in a four-game sweep.

Even-numbered years were good to the Giants. After a losing record in 2013, the Giants bounced back with another World Series run in 2014 against the Kansas City Royals.

During the 2022 season, shortstop Brandon Crawford moved into the all-time top ten in games played for the Giants.

Bumgarner was the hero with one of the greatest performances in playoff history. In his three World Series appearances he struck out 17 players and allowed only nine hits. His stunning five-inning relief effort in Game 7 earned him MVP honors and a third ring in five seasons.

The Giants were back in the playoffs in 2016 but lost a tough playoff NL Division Series to the Chicago Cubs. The team still had Posey, Bumgarner, shortstop Brandon Crawford, and first baseman Brandon Belt. But trades and injuries led to the Giants losing 98 games in 2017.

After four losing seasons, the Giants surprised all in 2021, winning a team record 107 games. While pitchers such as Kevin Gausman helped lead the way, Posey also had an All-Star season and Crawford was an MVP contender. The Giants lost in the playoffs but gave fans hope that they were back in contention to stay. Posey retired after the season, but it was time for a new generation of Bay Area stars to restore the glory.

TIMELINE

1883

The Giants play their first NL season as the New York Gothams.

1888

The Giants capture their first of two consecutive NL championships.

1905

Under manager John McGraw, the Giants win their fourth NL title and play in their first World Series, defeating the Philadelphia Athletics in five games.

1911

The Giants win their first of three NL titles in a row, but they lose all three World Series.

1921

The Giants win their first of four NL titles in a row and first of two World Series titles in a row.

1933

After an MVP season from pitcher Carl Hubbell, the Giants capture another World Series title in a five-game win over the Washington Senators.

1951

Bobby Thomson's famous "Shot Heard 'round the World" wins the NL title over the rival Brooklyn Dodgers, but the Giants lose in the World Series.

1954

An MVP season and "the Catch" from Willie Mays, help the Giants sweep Cleveland in the World Series.

1957

The Giants announce they are moving to San Francisco.

1962

The Giants reach the World Series but fall to the New York Yankees in seven games.

1989

The Giants reach the World Series, but it's halted for 10 days by an earthquake. The Oakland A's win a four-game sweep.

1992

Owner Peter Magowan buys the Giants and keeps them from moving to Florida. He then signs superstar outfielder Barry Bonds.

2001

Bonds hits 73 home runs to set the single-season MLB record.

2002

The Giants return to the World Series but lose in seven games to the Anaheim Angels.

2007

Bonds breaks Hank Aaron's career home-run record.

2010

After winning the NL West on the last day of the season, the Giants defeat the Texas Rangers in five games in the World Series.

2012

San Francisco sweeps the Detroit Tigers to capture another World Series.

2014

Madison Bumgarner's pitching leads the Giants to a third World Series title in five seasons.

2021

The Giants surprise fans by setting a team record with 107 wins after four consecutive losing seasons.

TEAM FACTS

FRANCHISE HISTORY

New York Gothams (1883–1884)
New York Giants (1885–1957)
San Francisco Giants (1958–)

WORLD SERIES CHAMPIONSHIPS

1905, 1921, 1922, 1933, 1954, 2010, 2012, 2014

KEY PLAYERS

Barry Bonds (1993–2007)
Madison Bumgarner (2009–19)
Orlando Cepeda (1958–66)
Will Clark (1986–93)
Brandon Crawford (2011–)
Carl Hubbell (1928–43)
Juan Marichal (1960–73)
Christy Mathewson (1900–16)
Willie Mays (1951–52, 1954–72)
Willie McCovey (1959–73, 1977–80)
Mel Ott (1926–47)
Buster Posey (2009–21)
Bill Terry (1923–36)

KEY MANAGERS

Dusty Baker (1993–2002)
Bruce Bochy (2007–19)
Leo Durocher (1948–55)
John McGraw (1902–32)

HOME STADIUMS

Polo Grounds I (1883–88)
Oakdale Park (1889)
St. George Cricket Grounds (1889)
Polo Grounds II (1889–90)
Polo Grounds III (1891–1957)
Hilltop Park (1911)
Seals Stadium (1958–59)
Candlestick Park (1960–99)
  Also known as:
  3 Com Park (1996–99)
Oracle Park (2000–)
  Also known as:
  Pacific Bell Park (2000–03)
  SBC Park (2004–05)
  AT&T Park (2006–18)

TEAM TRIVIA

NL GOAT

The 1930 Giants set an MLB record with a .319 team batting average. First baseman Bill Terry hit .401, making him the most recent NL player to have a batting average of at least .400.

SPLASH HITS

One of the unique aspects of the Giants' current home is its location right up against San Francisco Bay. This allows hitters to deposit home runs to right field into the water. Fans take boats and kayaks into McCovey Cove, often with fishing nets, in hopes of catching a homer.

HALL OF GIANTS

As of the 2022 class, the Giants had 26 players inducted into the Hall of Fame—the most of any NL team.

RACE TO 10K

In 2005 the Giants became the first MLB team to win 10,000 games. As of 2022, they ranked first for all-time in wins at more than 11,300.

GLOSSARY

ace

A team's top pitcher.

closer

A pitcher who comes in at the end of the game to secure a win for his team.

comeback

Going from losing a game to winning it.

contract

An agreement to play for a certain team.

debut

First appearance.

expansion

The addition of new teams to a league.

minor league

A developmental level of baseball below the major leagues.

pennant

Another name for a league championship; in MLB, refers to winning either the American or National League.

rookie

A first-year player.

save

When a relief pitcher comes in to finish a close game and secures a win.

screwball

A pitch that drops down and in the opposite direction to a curveball.

shutout

A complete game in which a team allows no runs.

veteran

A player who has played for many years.

MORE INFORMATION

BOOKS

Flynn, Brendan. *The MLB Encyclopedia*. Minneapolis, MN: Abdo Publishing, 2022.

Gitlin, Marty. *MLB*. Minneapolis, MN: Abdo Publishing, 2021.

Hewson, Anthony K. *GOATs of Baseball*. Minneapolis, MN: Abdo Publishing, 2022.

ONLINE RESOURCES

Booklinks
NONFICTION NETWORK
FREE! ONLINE NONFICTION RESOURCES

To learn more about the San Francisco Giants, please visit **abdobooklinks.com** or scan this QR code. These links are routinely monitored and updated to provide the most current information available.

INDEX

ABOUT THE AUTHOR

Douglas Carl is a retired English teacher, writer, and lifelong baseball fan.

THE BEST OF WORLD SOCCER

THE BEST TEAMS OF WORLD SOCCER

BY JON MARTHALER

SportsZone

An Imprint of Abdo Publishing
abdobooks.com

abdobooks.com

Published by Abdo Publishing, a division of ABDO, PO Box 398166, Minneapolis, Minnesota 55439.

Printed in the United States of America, North Mankato, Minnesota.
102023
012024

THIS BOOK CONTAINS RECYCLED MATERIALS

Cover Photo: Javier Soriano/AFP/Getty Images
Interior Photos: Alex Livesey/Allsport/Getty Images Sport/Getty Images, 4–5; Christian Liewig/TempSport/Corbis Sport/Getty Images, 6; Alex Livesey/Danehouse/Getty Images Sport/Getty Images, 8; Gonzalo Arroyo Moreno/Getty Images Sport/Getty Images, 10; Eric Alonso/Getty Images Sport/Getty Images, 11; Chris Brunskill/Fantasista/Getty Images Sport/Getty Images, 13; Markus Gilliar/GES Sportfoto/Getty Images Sport/Getty Images, 14; Simon Bruty/Allsport/Hulton Archive/Getty Images, 16–17; Harry How/Getty Images Sport/Getty Images, 18; Manuel Velasquez/Getty Images Sport/Getty Images, 20; Leopoldo Smith/Getty Images Sport/Getty Images, 22; Brad Smith/ISI Photos/Getty Images Sport/Getty Images, 24; Pictorial Parade/Archive Photos/Getty Images, 26; Harriet Lander/Copa/Getty Images Sport/Getty Images, 28–29; Jonathan Moscrop/Getty Images Sport/Getty Images, 30; Ryan Pierse/Getty Images Sport/Getty Images, 31; Mike Hewitt/Getty Images Sport/Getty Images, 32; Alex Livesey/Getty Images Sport/Getty Images, 34; Hulton Picture Library/Allsport/Hulton Archive/Getty Images, 36–37; Dave Cannon/Allsport/Hulton Archive/Getty Images, 38; Jamie McDonald/Getty Images Sport/Getty Images, 40; Elsa/Getty Images Sport/Getty Images, 42; Christof Koepsel/Bongarts/Getty Images, 44

Editor: Luke Hanlon
Series Designers: Karli Kruse and Joshua Olson

Library of Congress Control Number: 2023939436

Publisher's Cataloging-in-Publication Data

Names: Marthaler, Jon, author.
Title: The best teams of world soccer / by Jon Marthaler
Description: Minneapolis, Minnesota: Abdo Publishing, 2024 | Series: The best of world soccer | Includes online resources and index.
Identifiers: ISBN 9781098292294 (lib. bdg.) | ISBN 9798384910237 (ebook)
Subjects: LCSH: Soccer--Juvenile literature. | Professional sports--Juvenile literature. | Soccer Teams--Juvenile literature. | Soccer matches--Juvenile literature. | Soccer--Records--Juvenile literature.
Classification: DDC 796.334--dc23

TABLE OF CONTENTS

CHAPTER 1

EUROPE'S FINEST MEN'S TEAMS

Manchester United was so close. The Red Devils were trying to achieve something no other club from England had ever done: win three championships in one year. This is known as winning the "treble." The final step in this quest took place on May 26, 1999. By then United had already

Manchester United players pose for a team photo before the 1999 Champions League final.

won the Premier League, which is the top men's league in England. Shortly after, the team claimed victory in the Football Association (FA) Cup. That famous tournament includes teams from all levels of English men's soccer. Over many months, they face off in a knockout-style competition. Now, to clinch the treble, United had to beat Bayern Munich in the European Champions League final.

Each competition for the treble has unique challenges. In the Champions League, the best clubs from across Europe compete to become European champion. These teams are often the best in the world. And Bayern Munich had long been the dominant team in Germany.

Bayern Munich scored in the first six minutes. The game remained 1–0 into stoppage time. United's treble appeared doomed. Then, in the 91st minute, Teddy Sheringham tied the game for United. Two minutes later, Ole Gunnar Solskjær added another goal. Both strikers had come into the game as substitutes. Now they were the heroes as United held on to win 2–1 and claim the first treble for an English team.

It was a historic moment in English soccer. For United, it was the next great accomplishment in the team's rich history. Soccer had been invented in England in 1863, and men's club teams began forming soon after. United played its first season

Teddy Sheringham celebrates his game-tying goal in the 1999 Champions League final.

in England's First Division in 1892–93. In 1968 the Red Devils became the first English team to win a European title. Then, in the 1990s, the team from northwest England became a global force. United achieved so much that their home stadium, Old Trafford, became known as the "Theatre of Dreams."

The Premier League was founded in 1992–93. Under manager Alex Ferguson, United won 13 Premier League titles through 2013. The Red Devils also won two Champions League titles. Those United teams featured some of the biggest names in the sport, including David Beckham, Wayne Rooney, and Cristiano Ronaldo. When put together, all of this led to Manchester United becoming not just a dominant team but also one of the most popular teams in any sport in the world.

ENGLISH TRADITION

Manchester United set a new standard for English soccer during the 1990s and early 2000s. By then the sport had roots in the country going back more than a century. Clubs such as Arsenal, Aston Villa, Everton, Nottingham Forest, and Sunderland enjoyed periods of success. But no team was more dominant than Liverpool in the 1970s and 1980s. From 1976 to 1990, Liverpool won the English league title 10 times. The Reds didn't just dominate in England, though. They also won the European Cup four times during that run, in 1977, 1978, 1981,

ARSENAL'S INVINCIBLES

English club Arsenal has enjoyed periods of success over its long history. Its best season was in 2003–04. The London team went an entire Premier League season without a loss. It was the first time since 1889 that a team from England had gone undefeated. That Arsenal team became known as "The Invincibles."

and 1984. Since 1992, that tournament has been called the Champions League.

After 1990 it took a long time for Liverpool to win the English league title again. But the Reds won the Champions League in 2005 and 2019. They also added three FA Cup titles from 1992 to 2006. Led by dynamic wingers Mohamed Salah and Sadio Mané, Liverpool then ran away with the Premier League in 2020. That was Liverpool's 19th league title, which is the second most in England. While Manchester United has had more success in the league, no other English team has won as many as Liverpool's six European championships.

Mohamed Salah, *left*, and Sadio Mané combined to score 37 league goals in the 2019–20 season.

SPANISH ROYALTY

The first European Cup was held in the 1955–56 season. Superstar forward Alfredo Di Stéfano scored in the final to help Spanish club Real Madrid win the European crown. For the next four years, Di Stéfano scored in every European Cup final. And Real Madrid won each time. That streak ended in the 1961 European Cup. But no club has dominated the tournament like Real Madrid. The Spanish side won the European title for the 14th time in 2022. That was twice as many as any other team.

The club known as *Los Blancos* ("The Whites") has long been a powerhouse in the Spanish league, too. The constant winning has led millions of people around the world to root for Real Madrid. As of 2023, no team had more followers on social media than Real.

It also helps that Real Madrid often features some of the biggest stars in the world. During the late 1950s and early 1960s, the team featured the dominant forward line of Di Stéfano and Ferenc Puskás. The early 2000s "Galácticos" teams were loaded with stars such as Zinedine Zidane, Ronaldo Nazario, and David Beckham. A decade later, forwards Cristiano Ronaldo and Karim Benzema continued the tradition. Those two went on to be the top two goal scorers in the club's history. They also won four Champions League titles together. Even after Ronaldo left, Benzema lifted Real Madrid to another

Cristiano Ronaldo does his signature celebration after scoring one of his 451 goals for Real Madrid.

European title in 2022. Real Madrid surrounded him with other superstars like midfielder Luka Modrić and winger Vinicius Júnior. An intense rivalry with Barcelona helped Real Madrid stay sharp, too. The two teams have traditionally dominated Spanish soccer. Real Madrid players knew that if they ever let up, its biggest rival was ready to take advantage.

Barcelona plays in the Catalonia region of Spain. To its fans, the team represents that region and its values. Barcelona also stood up for common people when Spain was ruled by a dictator. That's in part why the team's motto is *"Més que un club,"* which means "More than a club." Real Madrid is Spain's most successful club. But usually if Real Madrid doesn't win La Liga, Spain's top league, Barcelona does. On top of its success in Spain, Barcelona has claimed five European titles. The Catalonian club has also done something its rivals have not. In 2009 and 2015, Barcelona won La Liga, the Copa del Rey, and the Champions League to complete the treble.

Lionel Messi was the main reason. The Argentine joined the club's famous youth academy as a boy. After making his debut for the senior team at 17, the forward became a star for Barcelona. Many now consider him the greatest player ever. Messi dazzled Barcelona fans for 17 years. His brilliant play led Barcelona to 35 trophies during his time with the club, including four Champions League titles.

While many world-class players have played for Barcelona, none have had a bigger impact on the club than Lionel Messi.

ITALIAN GIANTS

The best soccer in the world in the late 1980s and early 1990s was played in Italy. The country has always been dominated by three teams from two cities. The first is Juventus, which plays in Turin. The other two are from Milan: AC Milan and Internazionale, which is known as Inter Milan.

Each team has its own claim to fame. Through 2023, Juventus had won 36 Italian titles. AC Milan had seven European titles. Inter has had success in Italy and Europe.

Anchored by defender Giorgio Chiellini, Juventus finished the 2011–12 season undefeated to win its first title in nine years in Serie A, the top league in Italy. Then it won eight more in a row. At the time, that was the most consecutive titles for any team in a major European soccer league.

AC Milan's best era was from 1988 to 1996. Led by center backs Franco Baresi and Paolo Maldini, Milan won the European Cup three times and made it to five finals. Milan also won five league titles during this era. This included an undefeated season in 1991–92.

Inter split off from AC Milan in 1908. Since then, the two rivals have each enjoyed success. In 2021–22, AC Milan claimed its 19th league title. That tied Inter for the second most, behind Juventus. Inter's greatest period was from 2006 to 2010, as it won Serie A five years in a row. Then, in 2010, legendary

Juventus captain Giorgio Chiellini raises the Serie A trophy in 2019 to celebrate the team's eighth straight Italian league championship.

manager José Mourinho led Inter to the only treble by an Italian team.

DOMESTIC DOMINANCE

Each European country has its own men's soccer league. In many countries, one or two teams have emerged as the traditional powers. In Germany that team is Bayern Munich. The team won the Bundesliga, Germany's top league, for the 11th time in a row in 2023. That gave the team from southern

Germany 33 league titles. No other team has come close to matching that total.

Bayern Munich has not gone four straight years without winning the championship since the 1970s. On top of winning in Germany, Bayern has also won the European title six times.

Jamal Musiala, *center*, celebrates scoring a goal on the final day of the 2022–23 season to secure the Bundesliga title for Bayern Munich.

TOTALLY AJAX

In the 1960s and 1970s, Dutch club Ajax invented a new way to play. All of its players learned to play every position. Before this, most players usually stayed in only one area of the field. The Dutch system became known as "Total Football." Ajax used it to win three European Cups in a row from 1971 to 1973. The club's groundbreaking style has influenced all of soccer.

In 2013 and 2020, those titles completed trebles. Bayern has been so good for so long that German fans made a new word for the team: *Bayerndusel*. *Dusel* means "luck" in German. Other teams' fans are frustrated because no matter what happens, it seems like Bayern always wins.

Many other countries have one, two, or three dominant teams. Through 2023, AFC Ajax had won 36 league titles in the Netherlands. FC Porto, Benfica, and Sporting collectively claimed 87 titles in Portugal. In Scotland, Rangers had won 55 league titles, and Celtic had won 53. While new teams emerge as contenders across Europe every season, many of the continent's dominant teams have continued to win again and again.

CHAPTER 2

CLUBS AROUND THE WORLD

A driving rain fell on Foxboro, Massachusetts, on October 20, 1996. That didn't seem to bother the team used to the sunshine. Major League Soccer (MLS) had launched that year. And the Los Angeles Galaxy appeared on their way to victory in the first MLS Cup. In front of 34,643 fans, the Galaxy

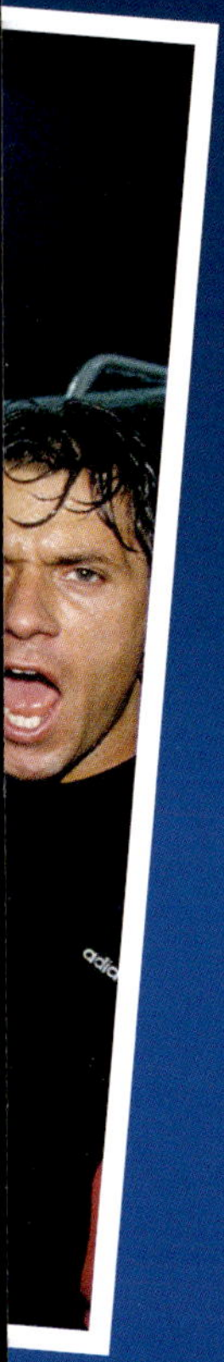

DC United players celebrate winning the very first MLS Cup in 1996.

took a 2–0 lead in the 56th minute. That's when DC United charged back.

Tony Sanneh scored in the 73rd minute. Shawn Medved tied the game eight minutes later. Then, in extra time, star defender Eddie Pope scored a "golden goal" to secure the league's first championship for DC United.

Soon after English students created modern soccer in the mid-1800s, the game began spreading around the world. Today it's played in more than 100 countries from every corner of the world—by men and by women. While the top club teams are usually found in Europe, great leagues and great teams can be found anywhere.

In North America, DC United emerged as the first dynasty in MLS. The team won three of the first four MLS Cups. It also won the regional championship in 1998. That tournament is now the CONCACAF Champions League, and it features the top teams of North and Central America.

Eventually United's opponent from that 1996 MLS Cup became the league's new powerhouse. The Galaxy won MLS titles in 2002 and 2005. Then, in 2007, it shocked the world by signing David Beckham. The English midfielder was one of the most popular players ever. It took some time for the team to build a winner around Beckham. But with teammates such as Landon Donovan and Robbie Keane, the Galaxy added back-to-back championships in 2011 and 2012. Even after Beckham left, the Galaxy won again in 2014. No team has more than the Galaxy's five MLS Cup titles.

The Seattle Sounders joined the league in 2009 and had consistent success right away. From 2009 to 2021, they never missed the playoffs. In a five-year span from 2016 to 2020, the Sounders made the MLS Cup four times and won it twice. They also won the CONCACAF Champions League in 2022.

A new team was challenging the Galaxy and the Sounders for West Coast dominance in the late 2010s. Los Angeles FC

David Beckham's arrival helped the Los Angeles Galaxy become the most recognized team in MLS.

(LAFC) joined MLS in 2018. The team featured Mexican forward Carlos Vela. He immediately became one of the league's most dangerous attacking players. LAFC proved to be a regular threat during the regular season. Finally, in 2022, the team broke through for an MLS Cup title. LAFC had taken over as the power of Los Angeles—and of MLS.

MEXICO'S BIG FOUR

Mexico's Liga MX has always been the most successful men's soccer league in North America. Its four best teams are called

AL-HILAL

In 2021 Al-Hilal of Saudi Arabia won the Asian Champions League for the fourth time. No other team in Asia can boast such a feat. A year later, Al-Hilal won its 18th Saudi league title, which was by far the most in the league's history.

Club América players celebrate scoring during a Liga MX game in 2018.

Los Cuatro Grandes. This means "The Big Four." Those teams are Club América, Cruz Azul, Pumas, and Chivas.

Mexico City is the biggest city in North America. In addition to having the most people, it also has the most money of any city in Mexico. Its soccer teams are some of the richest in Mexico. They also have the most fans.

The richest of all the teams in Mexico City is Club América. One of the nicknames for the club is the "Millionaires." This is because it spent so much money on new players in the 1960s. The club had its most successful era in the 1980s, however, as América won Liga MX five times from 1984 to 1989.

Club América is the team of the millionaires. But Cruz Azul is known as the team of the workers. The team was started by workers at a cement company. It eventually became a power. From 1970 to 1974, the team won the league title four times. It also won the CONCACAF title three times.

Since then Cruz Azul has lost a lot of big games. Many of these losses were surprising and painful for fans. Mexicans have coined a word: *cruzazulear*. It means "losing a game after victory is practically assured."

Pumas is the team of the National University of Mexico, called UNAM. Pumas started as the college team. But Pumas became a competitive professional team in 1954. Because of this, Pumas is known as the team of the young people in Mexico City. One such youngster was Hugo Sánchez. The forward started playing for the club's senior team as a teenager. Sánchez then helped Pumas win league titles in 1977 and 1981. Regarded as one of the best players in the history of Liga MX, Sánchez scored 97 goals in 188 games for Pumas.

Chivas plays in Guadalajara, the second-biggest city in Mexico. Though the club's name is C.D. Guadalajara, everyone calls the team "Chivas," which means "goats." In 1948 a reporter wrote that the team "plays like hopping goats." It was meant as an insult. But the name stuck.

Pumas players celebrate winning a game in 2021.

Chivas is known for fielding only players who are from Mexico. From 1957 to 1965, the team won seven titles in nine years. That included four in a row from 1959 to 1962. No other team in Mexico has been able to match that feat.

Although those four teams dominated Liga MX for years, new teams have emerged. CF Monterrey and Tigres UANL both play north of Mexico City in Monterrey. And they each became powers in the 2000s, winning multiple Liga MX and CONCACAF Champions League titles.

LETHAL THORNS

Soccer, for much of its history, has been limited to men. In many countries, women were banned from playing altogether. This was the case in many countries famous for men's soccer, including England, Germany, and Brazil. That finally began changing in the 1970s and 1980s. Women's club soccer took decades to take hold. By the 2010s, however, the women's game had found real momentum.

The United States has long been the dominant team in international women's soccer. The National Women's Soccer League (NWSL) launched in 2013 to finally bring a stable women's club league to the country. The Portland Thorns soon showed just how popular the sport could be. No NWSL team has enjoyed greater fan support over the years. And those fans have had a lot to cheer for.

Canadian striker Christine Sinclair is international soccer's all-time leading scorer, male or female. When she isn't playing for her national team, she plays for Portland. Sinclair has played for the Thorns since the NWSL started and has lifted them to three league championships. That included the 2022 title with the help of a new star. That year, talented

American forward Sophia Smith became the youngest Most Valuable Player (MVP) in NWSL history. Smith scored in the championship game to help the Thorns win the league title.

Sophia Smith of the Portland Thorns celebrates scoring in the 2022 NWSL championship game.

AL-AHLY

Al-Ahly of Egypt is Africa's most successful men's club team. In 2005 Al-Ahly was at its best, as it went unbeaten in 46 matches. Al-Ahly won the African Champions League, the Egyptian league, and two cup competitions that season. The club's dominance didn't stop there. In 2023 Al-Ahly won the African Champions League for a record 11th time.

The North Carolina Courage also have won a lot of trophies. Starting in 2017, North Carolina won the NWSL Shield for three straight years. That trophy goes to the team with the best regular-season record. The Courage also defeated the Thorns 3–0 in the 2018 championship game. North Carolina won the title again in 2019.

SOUTH AMERICAN STARS

In the early 1900s, Santos was a small club that had some success in its local Brazilian league. Then, in 1956, a talented 15-year-old nicknamed Pelé arrived. He stayed with the club for nearly two decades and became one of the greatest players of all time. And he made Santos a household name.

Playing in São Paulo—the biggest city in the southern hemisphere—Santos became a power. The team peaked in 1962 and 1963. The all-Brazilian team won the Copa Libertadores in each year to become champion of

Pelé scored 643 goals for Santos and helped the Brazilian club become recognized around the world.

South America. Then it beat the top European team each year in the Intercontinental Cup. That, in effect, meant Santos was the world champion.

Recently two teams in Brazil have become the country's dominant forces. In 2022 Rio de Janeiro–based club Flamengo won the Copa Libertadores for the second time in four years. The two previous seasons, São Paulo club Palmeiras won the competition. That included a dramatic win in 2021. In that year's final, Palmeiras forward Deyverson scored in extra time to defeat Flamengo.

Often, a team from Argentina or Brazil wins the Copa Libertadores. A handful of teams from each country has had periods of success. But no team has dominated the tournament as much as Independiente. The Argentina-based club won the Copa Libertadores four times in a row from 1972 to 1975. The team then added its record seventh championship in 1984.

However, neighboring teams Boca Juniors and River Plate often dominate discussions about club soccer in Argentina. The Buenos Aires teams have one of the sport's fiercest rivalries. Each has also enjoyed a ton of success. Boca Juniors won the Copa Libertadores for a sixth time in 2007. Its crosstown rival hasn't been able to match that. But River Plate won Argentina's top-flight league title in 2023 for a record 38th time.

CHAPTER 3

CLUBS ON THE RISE

France started a professional women's league in 1974. Olympique Lyonnais, known as Lyon, won its first league title in 1991. That was just the beginning for Lyon. The French club went on to win many more titles, including 14 straight from 2007 to 2020.

Ada Hegerberg of Lyon lifts the Champions League trophy in 2022.

Most early European women's teams were independent. Lyon, on the other hand, was backed by an established men's team of the same name. This support helped the Lyon women become the best team in Europe. The team won back-to-back European Women's Champions League titles in 2011 and 2012. Two years later, the club signed Norwegian striker Ada Hegerberg.

With one of the world's most dangerous goal scorers, Lyon claimed five straight Champions League titles from 2016 to 2020. After conquering Europe again in 2022, Lyon had won eight Champions League titles.

GERMAN GIANTS

The UEFA Women's Cup, now known as the European Women's Champions League, began in 2001–02. German teams thrived in the early years. FFC Frankfurt won its fourth title in 2015. That came after VFL Wolfsburg lifted the trophy in 2013 and 2014. After winning its first league title in 2013, Wolfsburg went on to win six of the next 10 German championships.

By then other men's clubs had figured out that providing resources to a women's team could lead to great success. No team showed that as much as Barcelona. Though the women's team had existed for years, it didn't become professional until 2015. And whereas Lyon's men's team had been successful in France, Barcelona's men's team was a global power. When the club put its resources behind the women's team, the squad took off.

Led by world-class midfielder Alexia Putellas, Barcelona set a record by winning 62 consecutive games in the Spanish league. The run lasted from June 2021 to May 2023. During that time, Barcelona won its first Champions League title in 2021. Two years later, Barcelona added to its trophy collection when it overcame a 2–0 first-half deficit to beat German club Wolfsburg in the 2023 Champions League final.

FIFA, the governing body of world soccer, voted Barcelona midfielder Alexia Putellas the best women's player in the world in 2021 and 2022.

Chelsea's Sam Kerr, *midair*, celebrates scoring in the 2023 FA Cup final.

Perhaps the fastest-growing women's soccer league is in England. The country that invented soccer started a professional women's league in 1991. Arsenal won its first title in 1993. Heading into the 2003–04 season, the Gunners had won the league five times. That season Arsenal won its first of nine straight league titles. The Gunners won the Champions League in 2007, making them the first English team to do so.

The league began to shift after Chelsea hired manager Emma Hayes in 2012. A former assistant at Arsenal, Hayes

Eden Hazard helped Chelsea win Premier League titles in 2015 and 2017.

led Chelsea to its first league title in 2015. After another championship in 2018, Chelsea signed superstar forward Sam Kerr in 2020. After she joined the club, Chelsea won four league titles in a row.

NEW MONEY, NEW POWER

Tradition has long been an indicator of success in global soccer. Clubs that have been good for decades, like Real Madrid, Bayern Munich, and Manchester United, remain powerhouses. However, as the sport has grown, wealthy new owners have bought soccer teams and shifted the power in some leagues.

PARIS SAINT-GERMAIN

For years Paris lacked a successful men's club team. Then, in 2011, the government of Qatar bought Paris Saint-Germain (PSG). Before its new owners took over, PSG had won only two league titles. Starting in 2013, it won the league almost every year. The owners also spent heavily to bring in some of the sport's biggest names in Neymar, Kylian Mbappé, and Lionel Messi.

Manchester City fans display a banner at the expense of their crosstown rivals Manchester United after City won the Premier League title in 2012.

Their ability to spend a lot of money on new players has helped some teams break into the elite ranks.

In England, London-based Chelsea had long been a fashionable club. But the blues didn't become a power until Russian billionaire Roman Abramovich bought the team in 2003. Prior to then, Chelsea's last league championship had been in 1955. With new investment, Chelsea brought in expensive players such as striker Didier Drogba and winger

Eden Hazard. They helped Chelsea win the Premier League five times from 2005 to 2017. Chelsea also won the Champions League in 2012 and 2021.

Manchester City has taken that to another level. The royal family of Abu Dhabi bought the English club in 2008. Until that point, crosstown rival Manchester United had dominated England. City won the league title in 1968 and had been a mediocre team for decades after that. Under new ownership with billions of dollars to spend, that changed.

In 2011–12 the two Manchester teams battled all season for the Premier League title. It came down to the wire. City trailed Queens Park Rangers 2–1 as the final game of the season went into stoppage time. If City didn't win, United would be Premier League champions. Miraculously, City forwards Edin Džeko and Sergio Aguero both scored in stoppage time. City fans erupted with joy as their team stole the title away from their biggest rivals.

The team has only gotten better since. City went on to win six more league titles through 2023. Five of those came under manager Pep Guardiola. That included the 2017–18 team that became the first in Premier League history to record 100 points in a season. Buying Norwegian striker Erling Haaland helped City go on a treble-winning season in 2023, matching United's feat in 1999.

CHAPTER 4

CONQUERING THE WORLD

Despite being one of the smallest countries in South America, Uruguay hosted the first men's World Cup in 1930. The country's national team had won the gold medal at the 1924 and 1928 Olympics. So when organizers were deciding where to hold the first World Cup, Uruguay was a

The Uruguay squad poses for a photo during the 1930 World Cup.

natural choice. And Uruguay continued its winning ways, as it beat Argentina 4–2 in the final.

Uruguay wasn't done. Brazil hosted the World Cup in 1950. The tournament's last match featured the host country against Uruguay. The two nations played in front of a crowd of 200,000 fans. The stadium fell silent, however, when Uruguay upset the Brazilians 2–1 to win its second world title.

The defeat was heartbreaking for Brazil's players and fans. The team more than made up for it in years to come, though. Brazil has gone on to become the most successful team in world soccer. It is the only team to have played in all 22 men's World Cups. And it's the only country that has won the tournament five times.

Brazil's first run of dominance started in 1958 when Pelé played in his first World Cup. At just 17 years old, Pelé was already one of the world's best players. In 1970 he and Brazil earned a third World Cup title. Many consider that year's Brazilian team to be the best the game has ever seen.

Brazil's flair carried on through generations. By the 1990s and 2000s, the South American powerhouse was back to its best. Exciting attacking players such as Romário, Ronaldo, and Ronaldinho led Brazil to three straight World Cup finals, including wins in 1994 and 2002.

Mario Götze, *left*, celebrates scoring a goal in extra time of the 2014 World Cup final. Germany held on to win 1–0 to claim its fourth World Cup title.

forward Giuseppe Meazza, Italy won back-to-back world titles in 1934 and 1938. Decades later, Italy added to its trophy collection by taking down other European threats. Italy cruised past West Germany 3–1 in the 1982 World Cup final. Then, in 2006, Italy outlasted France in a penalty shootout to win its fourth world championship.

WOMEN'S INTERNATIONAL POWERS

The first Women's World Cup took place in 1991. Five years later, the Olympics hosted a women's soccer tournament for the first time. The result was the same in both new tournaments: the United States won each time.

The US women weren't always a power. Founded in 1985, the team failed to win any of its four games that year. An aggressive, fearless approach soon turned things around. The style was exemplified in many ways by Michelle Akers. She scored the first goal in the history of the US team in 1985.

SPAIN

Despite a rich history in men's soccer, Spain went decades without a major championship. A golden generation of players changed that by winning European titles in 2008 and 2012. In between, Spain won the 2010 World Cup. The squad was famous for its style of play, called "tiki-taka," which emphasized keeping possession with many short, accurate passes.

Megan Rapinoe tallied six goals and three assists to help lift the United States to its fourth Women's World Cup title in 2019.

She led all players at the 1991 World Cup with 10 goals. And later she transitioned from a dominant striker to become a bruising defensive midfielder. Her play was vital to the United States winning a second World Cup in 1999.

Since Akers, the United States has continued to produce elite offensive players. Mia Hamm became international soccer's leading scorer. She retired after leading the Americans to another Olympic gold medal in 2004. Abby Wambach eventually surpassed Hamm. Meanwhile, Carli Lloyd seemed to always score in the biggest moments. Her goals secured Olympic gold medals in 2008 and 2012. Then, in the 2015 World Cup final, Lloyd scored a hat trick in the winning US effort.

Wambach had retired by 2019, and Lloyd was coming off the bench. But behind Alex Morgan and Megan Rapinoe, the Americans were as strong as ever in winning a fourth World Cup. No country comes close to matching the United States' success in women's soccer.

BEST OF THE REST

The United States was at the top of the soccer world after winning the 1999 Women's World Cup on home soil. Soon after, Germany stepped in to cement its place as the next great women's soccer team. In 2003, the World Cup was moved to the United States on short notice. Behind star forward Birgit Prinz,

Birgit Prinz raises the Women's World Cup trophy in 2007. The victory made Germany the first team to win the tournament twice in a row.

the Germans were ready. She scored seven goals to lead her country to its first Women's World Cup title. The team gave up just four goals in its six games. Four years later, the Germans were even better. This time Prinz scored only five times. But goalie Nadine Angerer didn't allow a single goal as Germany won again.

Japan consistently made it to the Women's World Cup since the competition started. Before the 2011 tournament, Japan hadn't had a lot of success on the big stage. But that team was united after an earthquake and tsunami hit Japan three months before the World Cup. The team inspired the country when it went on a run to the final. Playing against the United States, team captain Homare Sawa scored her tournament-leading fifth goal in extra time to tie the game 2–2. Japan outlasted the United States in a shootout to become Asia's first World Cup champion. That core of players went on to second-place finishes at the 2012 Olympics and the 2015 World Cup.

CHINA

China made it to the Women's World Cup final in 1999 but lost a penalty shootout to the United States. While it has never won a World Cup, China has dominated in Asia. China won its ninth Asian championship in 2022. That included seven straight titles from 1986 to 1999.

GLOSSARY

CENTER BACK

A defender who plays in the middle among a team's defenders.

CLUB

The team a player competes with outside of his or her national team.

CUP

In soccer, a trophy given for winning a tournament or a name for the tournament itself.

DYNASTY

A team that has an extended period of success, usually winning multiple championships in the process.

FORWARD

Also called a striker, the player who plays nearest the opponent's goal.

HAT TRICK

Three or more goals by the same player in one game.

INTERNATIONAL

Significant beyond a single nation's borders; in soccer, often applied to competition between national teams.

SHOOTOUT

A series of penalty kicks held after extra time to decide who wins a game.

STOPPAGE TIME

Also known as injury time, a number of minutes tacked onto the end of a half for stoppages that occurred during play because of injuries, free kicks, and goals.

SUBSTITUTE

A player who does not start the match but who enters later to replace a teammate.

WINGER

An attacking midfielder who plays wide.

MORE INFORMATION

BOOKS

Hanlon, Luke. *The Best Matches of World Soccer.* Minneapolis, MN: Abdo Publishing, 2024.

Hewson, Anthony K. *GOATs of Soccer.* Minneapolis, MN: Abdo Publishing, 2022.

McDougall, Chrös. *The Best Rivalries of World Soccer.* Minneapolis, MN: Abdo Publishing, 2024.

ONLINE RESOURCES

Booklinks NONFICTION NETWORK
FREE! ONLINE NONFICTION RESOURCES

To learn more about world soccer teams, please visit abdobooklinks.com or scan this QR code. These links are routinely monitored and updated to provide the most current information available.

INDEX

ABOUT THE AUTHOR

Jon Marthaler has been a freelance sportswriter for more than 20 years. He has written nine sports books for kids about MLS, world soccer, and many other sports. Jon lives in Saint Paul, Minnesota, with his wife and their two kids.